YES WE DID!
THE ART EDITION

David Sanders
Jeffrey White

David Sanders and Jeffrey White

©2017
ISBN-13: 978-1979842341
ISBN-10: 1979842345

Jeff White Fitness Solutions
www.JeffWhiteFitnessSolutions.com
https://www.youtube.com/user/JWFitness1

Other Books by Jeffrey White and David Sanders

Yes We Did! Amazing Accomplishments in African American History
Volume I

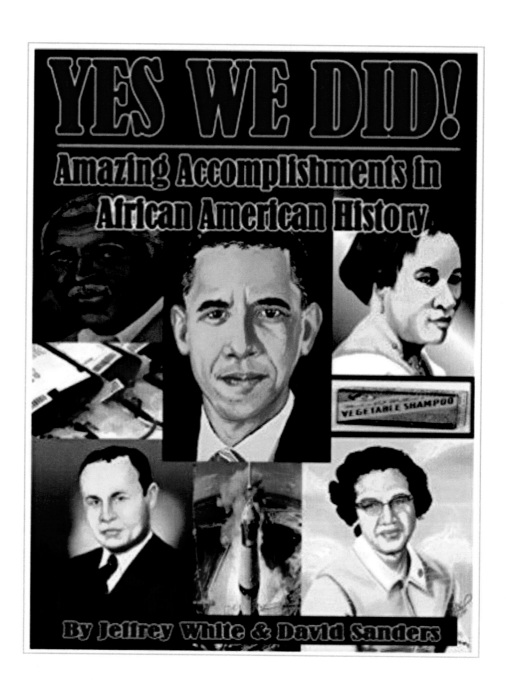

Other Books by Jeffrey White:

The 3 Pillars of Strength: Increasing Your Physical, Mental, and Spiritual Fitness.

Readi - Set Go! A Simple Guide to Establishing a Successful Small Business.

Co-written with Stephanie Wynn

Success Principles 101: A Step By Step Guide on Setting and Achieving Goals.

The Diet of Success: Healthy Eating Tips for Hard Working Professionals.

Foreword

This book is a celebration. A celebration of the brilliance and beauty of African American entertainers, politicians and scientists. The people on the following pages have affected each of us in their own ways. Some made us laugh, others made us think. Many improved the quality of our lives. All made us proud.

Revel in their achievements. Marvel at their desire to succeed. Be inspired by their hard work, sacrifice and dedication to be the best. It's time to celebrate. Yes we did!

Dedication

David Sanders:

Special Thanks to God from whom my talents flow. My father and mother: Willie L. Sanders Sr. and Leaon Sanders (RIP). My Wife Shantay Mitchell- Sanders and my children Cyla, Tia, Elisha and granddaughter Cyliah. My stepmom Casirene Collins –Sanders (RIP). My siblings Willie Jr., Evelyn, Edward, Tony, Lamar and Jamar. Walter Mitchell Jr. and Marcus Mitchell who always got my back. June Latham my heart (RIP). My art teacher Mr. Sherman Beck who taught me that its's better to take my time and be satisfied than to rush for a profit. My spiritual family who taught me faith and Mr. Jeff White who has been a friend forever! There are more but I only have so much space!

This book is also dedicated to all young African Americans. This is proof that you can accomplish anything you set your mind to if you believe in yourself and the power of teamwork!!

Dedication

Jeffrey White

As always, I must thank God first and foremost. I'm grateful for life and I thank Him for giving me the ability to write. I also thank my wife Monica for her unending support. Without her encouragement, this wouldn't be possible. I also dedicate this look to my son, Little Jeffrey. I hope to make you proud and inspire you to be the best you can be, at whatever you choose.

Dave, great work! Again!

This book is for anyone who's looking for something fresh, new and different. Dave and I are on a mission, and I hope you come along for the ride!

Contents

Section I:

The Entertainers

James Brown

Did you know?

- James Brown is affectionately known as the *"Godfather of Soul"*

- Brown's career lasted 50 years

- Rolling Stone ranked Brown #7 on its 100 greatest artist list of all time, and the most sampled artist of all time

- Brown received the following accolades and awards:

    o Grammy Awards – Lifetime Achievement award
    o UK Music Hall of Fame
    o Kennedy Center Honors
    o BET Awards – Lifetime achievement Award
    o Inducted into Rock & Roll Hall of Fame
    o Inducted into Georgia Music Hall of Fame
    o Star on Hollywood Walk of Fame
    o James Brown Boulevard and life-sized statue in Augusta, Georgia

- Brown was a firm believer in education:

    o In the 1960's, royalties from the song "Don't Be a Dropout" were donated to charities focused on student dropout prevention
    o In 2002, Brown created the *I Feel Good Foundation Inc. Trust* to provide scholarships to disadvantaged children and his grandchildren

"I just thank God for all the blessings."

"You can't teach others if you're living the same way."

"Like Christ said, 'love thee one another.' I learned to do that, and I learned to respect and be appreciative and thankful for what I had."

"Sometimes you struggle so hard to feed your family one way, you forget to feed them the other way, with spiritual nourishment. Everybody needs that." James Brown

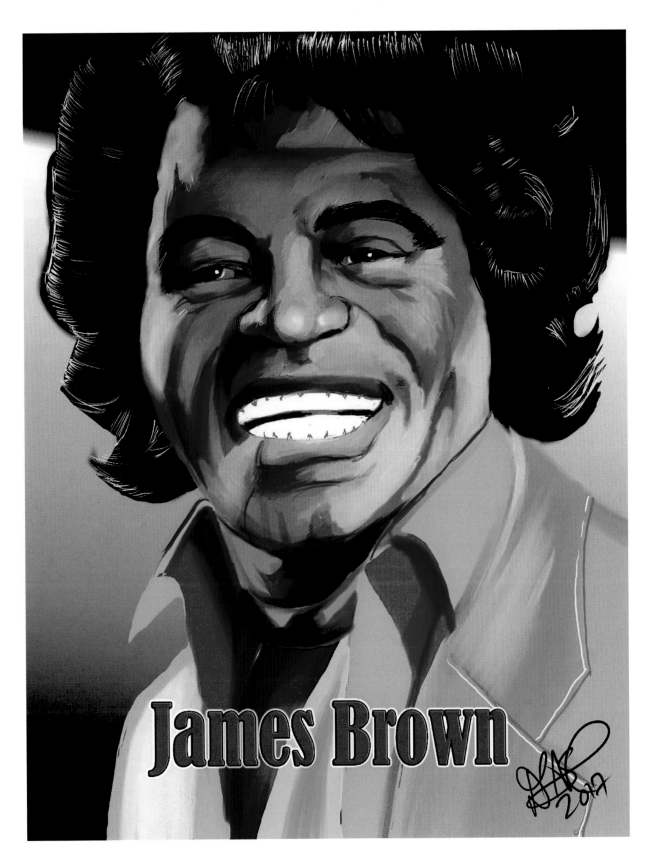

Bill Cosby

Did you know?

- William Henry Cosby is an actor, musician and stand-up comic

- His hit television series the Cosby Show, was the #1 sitcom in America from 1984-1989

- The popular animated series Fat Albert and the Cosby Kids ran from 1972-1985

- Over the course of his career, Cosby received the following awards:
  - Emmy Awards – 4
  - Grammy Awards – 10

- Cosby has been actively involved in the following charities:
  - Airlift Research Foundation
  - Hello Friend/Ennis William Cosby Foundation
  - Keep A Child Alive
  - Bob Woodruff Foundation
  - Robert F. Kennedy Memorial
  - Children's Miracle Network Hospitals
  - Jackie Robinson Foundation

- In 1988, Cosby donated $20 million to Spellman College

"In order to succeed, your desire for success should be greater than your fear of failure."

"The past is a ghost, the future a dream, all we have is now."

"I don't know the key to success, but the key to failure is trying to please everybody."

Dick Gregory

Did you know?

- Gregory was ranked #82 on Comedy Central's list of the 100 Greatest Stand-ups of all time

- Gregory has a star on the St. Louis Walk of Fame

- In 1965, Gregory joked about the Los Angeles Riots on the Merv Griffin Show: *"I'm standing on the corner, and there's this one guy running down the street with a couch on his back. So I say, 'Hey, buddy, are you a looter?' And he says, 'No, I'm a psychiatrist on my way to a house call.'"*

- Gregory led fund raisers to feed hungry people in Marks, Mississippi and visited Ethiopia to fight against world hunger

- In 1978, Gregory marched alongside Gloria Steinem and others in Washington D.C. to demand an extension of the proposed Equal Rights Amendment

"Love is man's natural endowment, but he doesn't know how to use it. He refuses to recognize the power of love because of his love for power."

"Fear and God do not occupy the same space."

"If you don't program your mind, it will be programmed for you." Dick Gregory

Taraji Henson

Did you know?

- Henson portrayed Katherine Johnson in the movie Hidden Figures, winning a Screen Actors Guild Award for Outstanding Performance by a Cast in a Motion Picture

- In 2016, Henson made the Time 100 list, being named one of the 100 most influential people in the world

- In 2015, Henson was named the 2015 Entertainer of the Year at the NAACP Image Awards

- Henson supports the following charities and foundations:
  - UNICEF
  - The Heart Truth
  - PETA Hope North
  - A Place Called Home

"I don't harp on the negative because if you do, then there's no progression. There's no forward movement. You got to always look on the bright side of things, and we are in control. Like, you have control over the choices you make."

"It's up to you to be responsible for how you feel if you're not happy. Your happiness lies in your hands. You can't rely on man to make you happy or complete. That starts with you."

"I never gave up even though others told me I wouldn't make it. I saw the bigger picture and I went after it." Taraji P Henson

Whitney Elizabeth Houston

Did you know?

- Whitney Houston sold more than 200 million records worldwide, making her one of the greatest selling recording artists of all time

- Houston had a record setting seven consecutive number one Billboard Hot 100 songs

- Houston created the Whitney Houston Foundation for Children, which cared for the homeless as well as children with cancer and AIDS

- In 1997, Houston raised over $300,000 from her HBO Concert Classic Whitney Houston live from Washington, D.C. for the Children's Defense Fund

- Houston donated all royalties from her 1991 rendition of the Star Spangled Banner to the American Red Cross

- Houston was an active supporter of the following charities:
    - The United Negro College Fund
    - The Special Olympics
    - Muhammad Ali Parkinson Center
    - American Foundation for AIDS Research

"We all die. The goal isn't to live forever, but to create something that will."

"There can be miracles when you believe."

"If I fail, if I succeed, at least I live as I believe." Whitney Houston

DL Hughley

Did you know?

- Hughley is an Original King of Comedy, along with Bernie Mac, Steve Harvey and Cedric the Entertainer

- Hughley was expelled from high school but eventually obtained his GED

- Hughley has appeared in over a dozen movies and television shows

- Hughley is a syndicated radio host, and can be heard in over 60 cities across the country

"Every group has its idiosyncrasies, but at a certain point we are all human."

"No matter how bad things are, you can at least be happy that you woke up this morning." D.L. Hughley

Michael Jackson

Did you know?

- Michael Jackson was known as the King of Pop

- Jackson was the eighth of ten children

- Jackson's album Thriller sold 65 million copies, making it the best-selling album of all time

- Jackson was inducted into the Rock & Roll Hall of Fame (not once, but twice)

- Jackson won more awards than any other recording artist in history, including 13 Grammy's and 26 American Music Awards

- In 2000, The Guinness World Records noted Jackson supported 39 charities, more than any other entertainer, including the following:

  - Big Brothers Big Sisters
  - United Negro College Fund
  - Make-A-Wish Foundation
  - End Hunger Network
  - American Cancer Society
  - Boys & Girls Clubs of America
  - Cure4Lupus
  - AIDS Project Los Angeles
  - Ronald McDonald House Charities
  - TJ Martell Foundation
  - YMCA
  - End Hunger Network

"In a world filled with hate, we must still dare to hope. In a world filled with anger, we must still dare to comfort. In a world filled with despair, we must still dare to dream. And in a world filled with distrust, we must still dare to believe."

"Please go for your dreams. Whatever your ideals, you can become whatever you want to become."

"It all went by so fast didn't it? I wish I could do it all over again, I really do." Michael Jackson

Michael Jackson

Bernie Mack

Did you know?

- Mac was an original King of Comedy, along with DL Hughley, Cedric the Entertainer and Steve Harvey

- Mac has appeared in dozens of films, and starred in the hit television show The Bernie Mac Show

- After his death, The Bernie Mac Foundation was created to bring awareness to Sarcoidosis, a mysterious disease that causes inflammation in the tissues

"You can't change what happened. Just like you can't change the future by worrying about it. You just have to keep moving."

"Suffering is a good teacher. It keeps you in its grip until you've learned your lesson."

"I can't build myself up by beating somebody else down." Bernie Mac

Prince

Did you know?

- Prince sold more than 100 million albums worldwide
- Prince used several pseudonyms throughout his career, including Jamie Starr and the Starr Company, Alexander Nevermind, Joey Coco and Christopher
- Prince played practically all the instruments on his first 5 albums
- Prince was a musical genius, mastering the guitar, drums, percussion, bass, keyboard, piano, and synthesizer while in his teens
- Prince played 27 instruments on his first album
- Prince was married to Matye Garcia from 1996-2000, and Manuela Testolini from 2001-2006

- Prince won the following awards:
  - Academy Award – 1
  - American Music Award – 4
  - BET Award – 1
  - Brit Award – 6
  - Golden Globe Award – 1
  - Grammy Award – 7
  - MTV Music Award – 4

- Prince was an active philanthropist, performing many charitable acts anonymously or with little fanfare:

  - Performed in a charity concert with Jay-Z, Beyonce and Nicki Minaj to raise money for Black Lives Matter in October 2015
  - Donated $250,000 to Eau Claire Promise Zone, a Columbia South Carolina organization helping preschoolers and their families
  - Donated $250,000 to the Uptown Dance Academy, allowing it to remain open in 2014
  - Donated $1 million to the Harlem's Children Zone, a non-profit assisting impoverished children and families
  - Donated $12,000 to the Louisville Free Public Library in 2001, enabling the first full service library for African Americans (Western Branch Library) to remain open
  - Donated $500,000 to Marva Collins and her Westside Preparatory School Teacher Training Institute in Chicago

"Sometimes it takes years for a person to become an overnight success."

"Do me a favor, and take care of each other, alright? It don't matter the color, we are all family."

"Hold on a second: If a black kid wears a hoodie, you say he's a thug, and if a white kid wears a hoodie, you say it's Mark Zuckerberg. Why is that? We just haven't produced enough black Mark Zuckerbergs. Why don't we focus on that?" Prince

Richard Pryor

Did you know?

- Both Rolling Stone and Comedy Central ranked Pryor as the #1 stand-up comic of all time

- Pryor received the Grammy Lifetime Achievement Award in 2006

- Between 1967 and 2003, Pryor appeared in over 50 movies and released 20 albums

- In 1988, Pryor won the first Mark Twain Prize for American Humor

- Dave Chappelle, Chris Rock, Sam Kinison, Jerry Seinfeld, Eddie Murphy, Martin Lawrence, George Carlin, Eddie Griffin, Patrice O'Neal, Jon Steward and Eddie Izzard all credit Pryor as an influence on their decisions to become comics

- Pryor was an animal lover, who was opposed to the cruelty and mistreatment of animals: The People for the Ethical Treatment of Animals (PETA) give an award in his name annually to individuals who have worked to prevent the cruelty to animals and animal suffering

"Two things people throughout history have had in common are hatred and humor. I am proud that I have been able to use humor to lessen people's hatred."

"Sure, I have friends, plenty of friends, and they all come around wantin' to borrow money. I've always been generous with my friends and family, with money, but selfish with important stuff like love."

"I believe the ability to think is blessed. If you can think about a situation, you can deal with it. The big struggle is to keep your head clear enough to think." Richard Pryor

Denzel Washington

Did you know?

- Washington is a Christian and reads the Bible daily

- Washington has served as the national spokesperson for the Boys and Girls Clubs of America

- Washington has won the following awards:
    - Academy Awards - 2
    - Golden Globe Awards – 3
    - Tony award - 1
    - NAACP Image Awards - 17
    - MTV awards – 2
    - Screen Actors Guild Awards - 1
    - Film Critic Award - 19
    - Black Reel Awards – 6

- Washington actively supports the following charities:

    - Keep A Child Alive
    - Make – A Wish Foundation
    - Save Africa's Children
    - Nelson Mandela Children's Fund
    - Stand Up to Cancer
    - Cedars-Sinai Medical Center
    - Elton John AIDS Foundation
    - Artists for a New South Africa
    - Elevate Hope Foundation

"I made a commitment to completely cut out drinking and anything that might hamper me from getting my mind and body together. And the floodgates of goodness have opened upon me – spiritually and financially."

"Everything you think you see in me, everything I've accomplished… Everything that I have is by the grace of God."

"Don't aspire to make a living, aspire to make a difference." Denzel Washington

Oprah Winfrey

Did you know?

- Winfrey's birth certificate says "Orpah," but people kept calling her "Oprah"

- At age 13, Winfrey ran away from home and became pregnant at age 14

- A 17 year old Winfrey won the Miss Black Tennessee beauty pageant

- A young Winfrey was fired from WJZ in Baltimore because they felt she was *"dull and stiff on the air and regularly mispronounced words."*

- CNN and Time.com said Winfrey was *"arguably the world's most powerful woman."*

- Winfrey is the richest self-made woman in America and the first woman black billionaire in the world

- Winfrey has given more than $400 million to various charities and causes:

    - 400 scholarships to Morehouse College
    - $12 million donation to the Smithsonian's National Museum of African History and Culture
    - Established the Oprah Winfrey Leadership Academy for Girls in Johannesburg, South Africa
    - Ranked among the top 50 most generous Americans

"Lot's of people want to ride with you in the limo, but what you want is someone who will take the bus with you when the limo breaks down."

"Surround yourself with people who are only going to take you higher."

"Be thankful for what you have; you'll end up having more. If you concentrate on what you don't have, you will never, ever have enough." Oprah Winfrey

Section II

The Scientists & Inventors

This page intentionally left blank.

Benjamin Banneker

Did you know?

- Banneker taught himself astronomy and predicted a solar eclipse in 1789

- In 1791, Banneker was recruited to help create the boundaries of Washington D.C.

- Banneker's grandmother used the Bible to teach him how to read and write

"The colour of the skin is in no way connected with strength of the mind or intellectual powers."
Benjamin Banneker

Benjamin Banneker

Dr. Patricia Bath

Did you know?

- Dr. Patricia Bath is an ophthalmologist who received a patent for her laser device that removed cataract lenses

- Dr. Bath has four patents

- Dr. Bath is the first African American woman to receive a patent for medical purposes

"Do not allow your mind to be imprisoned by majority thinking. Remember that the limits of science are not the limits of imagination." Dr. Patricia Bath

Patricia Bath

George Carruthers

Did you know?

- Carruthers is physicist, space scientist and inventor

- In 1969, Carruthers created the "Image Converter," which detected electromagnetic radiation

- His cameras have been used on the space shuttle

- Carruthers created a camera that was placed on the moon in 1972

- Carruthers was inducted into the National Inventors Hall of Fame in 2003

"Failure is not in your vocabulary; rather, you convert all your working experiences, be they positive or negative, into fuel for future success." George Carruthers

George Carruthers

George Washington Carver

Did you know?

- Carver was a world-renowned inventor and botanist

- Carver discovered nearly 300 uses for the peanut

- In 1965, the USS George Washington Carver was launched, a nuclear powered fleet ballistic missile submarine

- The George Washington Carver National Monument was erected on July 14, 1943 in Missouri: the first national monument dedicated to an African American and the first to someone other than a president

"Where there is no vision, there is no hope."

"There is no shortcut to achievement."

"No individual has any right to come into the world and go out without leaving something behind."
George Washington Carver

George Crum

Did you know?

- Crum was a master chef for upscale restaurants in the 1800's

- Today's potato chip is believed to be derived from Crum's popular snack: the Saratoga Chips

Dr. Charles Drew

Did you know?

- Dr. Drew was a physician, master surgeon and researcher

- Dr. Drew is the first African American surgeon to be an examiner on the American Board of Surgery

- Dr. Drew came up with the idea of storing blood on refrigerated trucks, known today as the bloodmobile

- Dr. Drew has over a dozen educational institutions named after him, including elementary schools, high schools, medical schools, college dormitories and laboratories

"Excellence of performance will transcend artificial barriers created by man."

"I feel that the recent ruling of the United States Army and Navy regarding the refusal of colored blood donors is an indefensible one from any point of view. As you know, there is no scientific basis for the separation of the bloods of different races except on the basis of the individual blood types or groups." Charles R Drew

Thomas Elkins

Did you know?

- Thomas Elkins was a pharmacist

- In 1870, Elkins received a patent for a combination dining table, ironing table and quilting frame

- Elkins was an abolitionist (a person who fought for the ending of slavery)

- Elkins was the secretary of the Vigilance Committee, which provided food, clothing, money, legal assistance and temporary shelter for escaped slaves seeking freedom

Katherine Johnson

Did you know?

- Katherine Johnson's life and career at NASA was chronicled in the hit movie Hidden Figures (played by Taraji Henson)

- Johnson graduated high school at age 14

- In 1969, Johnson helped calculate the Apollo 11 flight to the moon

- Johnson has worked on the Space Shuttle Program and helped devise plans for future missions to Mars

"Math. It's just there… You're either right or you're wrong. That's what I like about it."

"I felt most proud of the success of the Apollo mission. They were going to the moon and I computed the path to get there." Katherine Johnson

John Lee Love

Did you know?

- On November 23, 1897 Love invented the pencil sharpener

- Love's invention was called the "Love Sharpener"

John Lee Love

Alexander Miles

Did you know?

- In 1887, Miles received a patent for the elevator

- In 1900, Miles was known as the *"wealthiest colored man in the Northwest"*

- Miles was inducted into the National Inventors Hall Of Fame in 2007

Garrett A. Morgan

Did you know?

- Morgan has several prominent inventions: the smoke hood (aka gas mask), a cream that could straighten hair, and the modern-day traffic signal

- Morgan is the first African American to own an automobile in Cleveland

- Morgan's smoke hood was used by U.S. troops in World War I

- Morgan was a Prince Hall Freemason

- Morgan helped found the Cleveland Association of Colored Men and donated money to HBCU's

"If you can be the best, then why not try to be the best?" **Garrett A. Morgan**

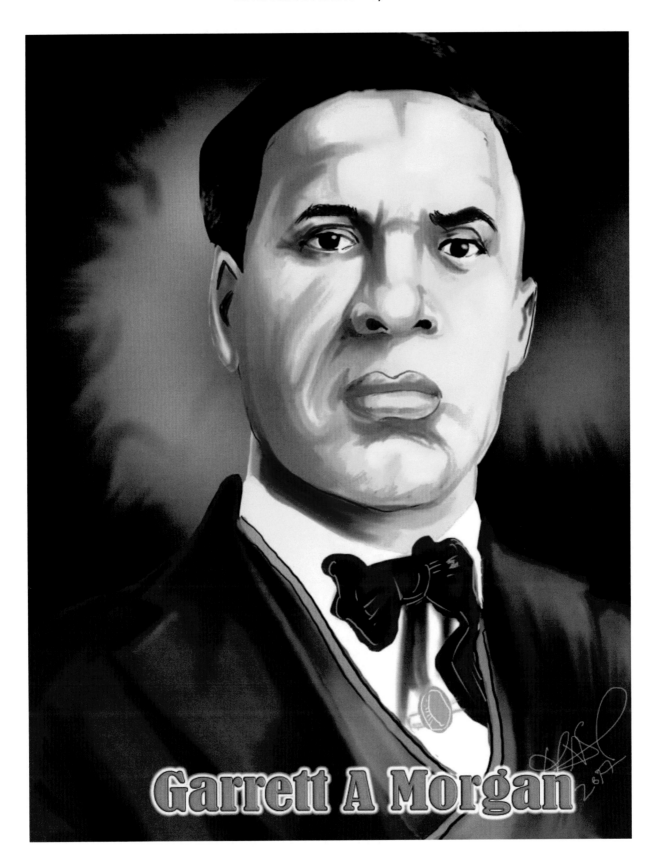

William Purvis

Did you know?

- On January 7, 1890, Purvis received a patent for the fountain pen

- Between 1884 and 1897, Purvis received 6 patents for a variety of inventions, including a hand stamp, electric railway switch and a magnetic car balancing device

"The object of my invention is to provide a simple, durable, and inexpensive construction of a fountain pen, adapted to general use, and which may be carried in the pocket." William B. Purvis

William Purvis

John Standard

Did you know?

- On June 14, 1891, Standard took the refrigerator and made it better by improving its functioning and efficiency

- Standard worked on the already existing oil stove and made it better, earning a patent that allowed it to be used to serve buffet style meals on trains, for the first time ever

"This invention relates to improvements in refrigerators; and it consists of certain novel arrangements and combinations of parts." John Standard

John Standard

Madame CJ Walker

Did you know?

- Walker revolutionized hair care for women of color in the early 1900's

- At the time of her death, Walker was the wealthiest African American woman in the United States

- Walker's sales team sold products in the United States, Cuba, Jamaica, Haiti, Panama, and Costa Rica

- Walker hired Vertner Tandy, the first black architect and founding member of Alpha Phi Alpha Fraternity Inc. to design her home in Irvington-on- Hudson, New York

"I am not satisfied in making money for myself. I endeavor to provide employment for hundreds of women of my race."

"There is no royal flower-strewn path to success. And if there is, I have not found it, for if I have accomplished anything in life it is because I have been willing to work hard."

"I had to make my own living and my own opportunity, but I made it! Don't sit down and wait for the opportunities to come. Get up and make them." Madam CJ Walker

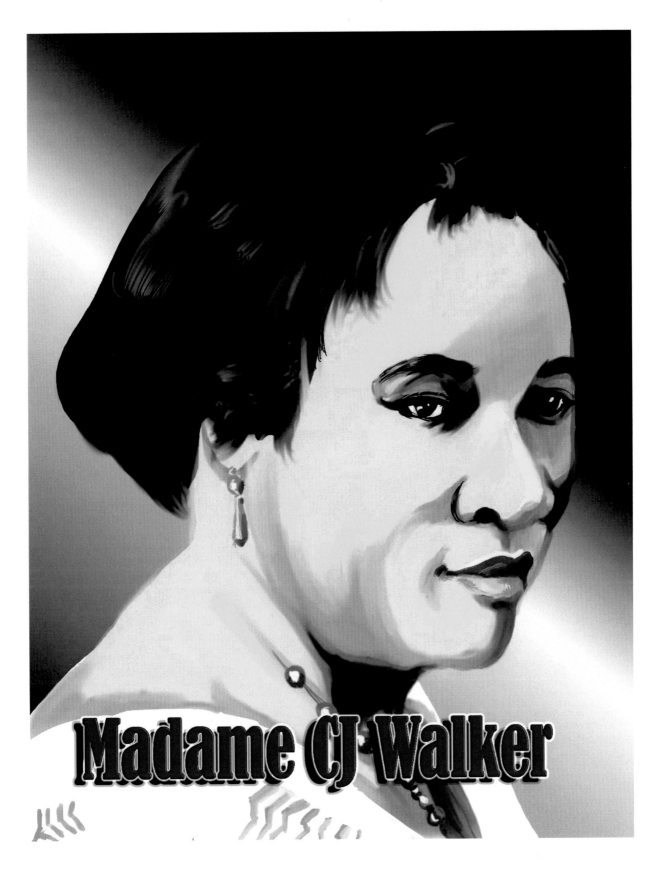

Granville Woods

Did you know?

- In 1878, Woods became the first African American to become a mechanical and electrical engineer

- Woods had close to 60 patents, earning him the nickname the "Black Thomas Edison"

- In 1885, Woods created the "telegraphony", an invention that allowed voice and telegraph messages to be sent over a single wire

Section III
The Politicians

This page intentionally left blank.

Carol Mosley Braun

Did you know?

- Mosley-Braun is the first female African American Senator, serving from 1993 to 1999

- Braun is the first woman to serve on the Senate Finance Committee

"It's not impossible for a woman – a black woman - to become President."

"We must invest in infrastructure development and rebuilding communities to create jobs."

"Magic lies in challenging what seems impossible."

"There are those who would keep us slipping back into the darkness of division, into the snake pit of hatred, of racial antagonism and of support for symbols of the struggle to keep African Americans in bondage." Carol Mosley Braun

Carol Moseley Braun

Thurgood Marshall

Did you know?

- Marshall is the first African American to serve on the on the United States Supreme Court

- Justice Marshall won an astounding 29 of 32 cases he took before the Supreme Court

- Before joining the Supreme Court, Marshall was a powerful civil rights attorney, playing a crucial role in the advancement of rights for African Americans

"The measure of a country's greatness is its ability to retain compassion in times of crisis."

"None of us got where we are solely by pulling ourselves up by our bootstraps. We got here because somebody – a parent, a teacher, an Ivy League crony or a few nuns – bent down and helped us pick up our boots."

"It's a democracy if we can keep it. And in order to keep it, you can't sit still. You must move, and if you don't move, they will run over you." Thurgood Marshall

Barack Obama

Did you know?

- In 2009, Obama became the first African American President of the United States

- Obama worked for Davis, Miner, Barnhill & Galland, a law firm specializing in civil rights from 1993 to 2004

- Obama graduated from Harvard Law School, and was the first black president of the Harvard Law Review

- Obama won the Nobel Peace Prize in 2009

- Obama and his wife Michelle have supported the follow charities:

  - Eracism Foundation
  - Harlem Children's Zone
  - K.I.D.S.
  - NAACP
  - National Domestic Violence Hotline
  - Save the Elephants
  - The Trevor Project
  - Human Rights First
  - Peace Players International

"If you run, you stand the chance of losing, but if you don't run you've already lost."

"The future rewards those who press on. I don't have time to feel sorry for myself. I don't have time to complain. I'm going to press on."

"If you're walking down the right path and you're willing to keep walking, eventually you'll make progress." Barack Obama

President Barack Obama

Hiram Revels

Did you know?

- In 1870, Hiram Revels became the first African American Senator in U.S. history

- Senator Revels was president of Alcorn College, the first land grant college for black students

- Revels helped organize two regiments of African American troops to fight for the Union in the Civil War

"I am true to my own race. I wish to see all done that can be done for their encouragement to assist them in acquiring property, in becoming intelligent, enlightened, useful, valuable citizens." Hiram Revels

Condoleezza Rice

Did you know?

- In 2005, Rice became the 66th Secretary of State of the United States, and the first African American woman to serve in this role

- Rice studied Russian at Moscow State University

- Rice graduated from college at age 19 with a B.A. in political science

- In 1992, Rice founded the Center for New Generation, an after-school program in East Palo Alto and Menlo Park California, designed to raise high school graduation rates

"My mom was a teacher. I have the greatest respect for the profession. We need great teachers, not poor or mediocre ones."

"Great leaders never accept the world as it was and always work for the world as it should be."

"If you are taught bitterness and anger, then you will believe you are a victim. You will feel aggrieved and the twin brother of aggrievement is entitlement. So now you think you are owed something and you don't have to work for it and now you're on a really bad road to nowhere because there are people who will play to that sense of victimhood, aggrievement and entitlement, and you still won't have a job."

"You can never cede control of your own ability to be successful to something called racism."
Condoleezza Rice

Section IV

Puzzles, Coloring Pages and Word Games

This page intentionally left blank.

Word Search # 1

The Entertainers

```
Y M C E I V D M Q G S T R I Y
H I I G C T N Q O P U O V D A
P C R S I N G E R O Y I E F A
R H D L U D I R K R N M T R W
U A E V A L Q R P L O W B A J
M E C F E P I D P C J Y A A R
E L S A B E R N I E M A C L M
I E O B Y A M N V Q B K R V K
L G N Q H J O U U R S A V A B
R N K C G V T O X O K O P B H
A A I F N C O I N N J P W T B
H R O K K N W B E H Q S M A V
C I L U V P N A F C J I R Y S
B O Y E N T I H W H V I E P N
O Q X S Y A I D W V O S O S X
```

BERNIEMAC
CEDRIC
CHARLIEMURPHY
COMEDY
GUITAR
JACKSON
MICHAEL
MOONWALK
MOTOWN
PRINCE
RICHARDPRYOR
SINGER
WHITNEY

Hint: Words can be horizontal, vertical, backwards or diagonal.

Word Scramble: The Entertainers

RICNEP

IURATG

HORNIOPEMC   (2)

SIACUMNI   (7)

VOETILISNE   (8)

RAGYMM

NOBYCEÉ   (9)

PORHA   (5)

IRNENTEAERT

RUMMERD

BEAKYROD   (3)

PAINO   (1)

DIANGNC   (6)

SUIMC   (4)

NOXPOHEAS

J _ _ _ _ _ _ (1 2 3 4 5 6)   F _ _ _ (7 8 9)

Unscramble each of the clue words.
Copy the letters in the numbered cells to other cells with the same number.

Crossword Puzzle: The Entertainers

Across	Down
2. Most sought after award in the music industry	1. Star of The Color Purple
8. movie starring Eddie Murphy and Richard Pryor	3. Beyoncé's singing group
10. Popular record label	4. Iconic movie named after a day of the week
11. married Whitney Houston	5. Owner of the 40-40 club
12. Has a radio show and several television shows	6. R&B group from Boston
14. Prince's favorite color	7. Has 88 keys
	9. son on the Cosby Show
	10. Michael Jackson's signature move
	13. Popular rapper born in Toronto

Who Am I? (Entertainment)

Unscramble the tiles to reveal famous musical groups

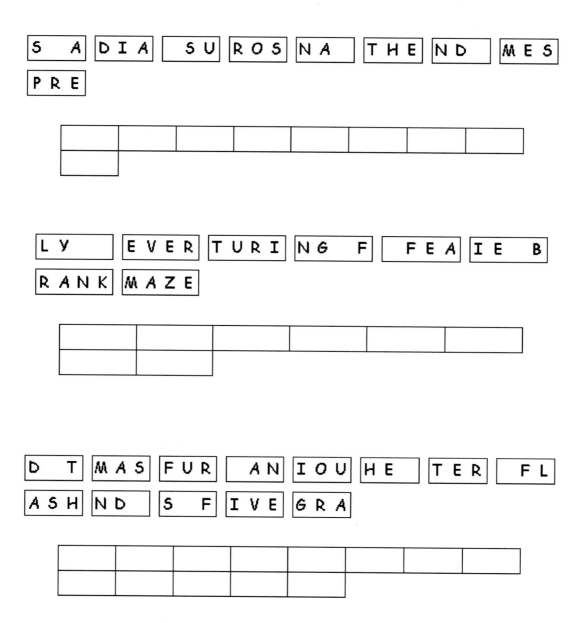

Word Search #2
Entertainment

```
T A R A J I P H E N S O N A A
R O Y R P D R A H C I R S C E
K J P Y N D L M S O Z A T A Y
C A H E A F J G E O D O L D D
A M U A C D O M R K R S E E O
B E I U R B G I U I R M R M O
Y S G T Q L H N G E O C C Y W
A B D Z F R E Y I C O H O A Y
P R F E T T O M F N M O I W L
G O G F N B Y O N C I T R A L
I W U V Y Z S U E I D A D R O
B N X B I G E L D X G W R D H
V X A R N H R L D I Q H X T Q
G B T I C E M P I R E S T L H
L F K Y M M E R H L O E U S I
```

ACADEMYAWARD - ACTOR - BABYBOY - BIGPAYBACK - COOKIE – DENZEL - EMMY - EMPIRE
HARLEMNIGHTS – HIDDENFIGURES – HOLLYWOOD – JAMESBROWN - KINGSOFCOMEDY
RICHARDPRYOR – TARAJIPHENSON - TRAININGDAY

Hint: Words can be horizontal, vertical, backwards or diagonal.

Discover the Phrase

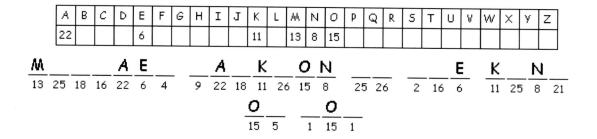

A	B	C	D	E	F	G	H	I	J	K	L	M	N	O	P	Q	R	S	T	U	V	W	X	Y	Z
22				6						11		13	8	15											

M _ _ A E _ _ _ A K _ O N _ _ _ _ E K _ N _
13 25 18 16 22 6 4   9 22 18 11 26 15 8   25 26   2 16 6   11 25 8 21

O _ _ O _
15 5   1 15 1

A	B	C	D	E	F	G	H	I	J	K	L	M	N	O	P	Q	R	S	T	U	V	W	X	Y	Z
				12									1	18			16								

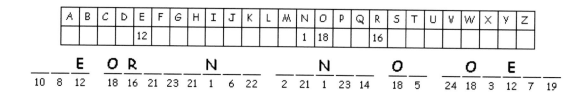

_ _ E _ O R _ _ N _ _ _ N _ O _ _ O E
10 8 12   18 16 21 23 21 1 6 22   2 21 1 23 14   18 5   24 18 3 12 7 19

A	B	C	D	E	F	G	H	I	J	K	L	M	N	O	P	Q	R	S	T	U	V	W	X	Y	Z
				15											20		19								

P R _ _ _ E _ _ _ R R E _ _ _ P _ R P _ E _ R _ _ _
20 19 2 7 14 15   24 21 1 19 19 15 22   2 7   20 10 19 20 17 15   19 1 2 7

Word Search #3

The History-Makers

```
P G S Q A P Z D R N Z U O M R
H E N N U T O F E L I P S X E
S U N R O O S B F I E S C H K
H T V C G I R N R G N B I E E
E I A R I T T K I M Y R E V N
S O U N X L V N G K A S N O N
V H I W D V S Y E M L Q C L A
T R E V R A C H R V U E E J B
E R G J C C R E A D N S D J T
D W O D H V V D T R J I U Z A
I O F H Z E L H O Z P J D X I
X G Q B L I J L R K D E U X C
C Z F S E L E V A T O R N V E
N E P N I A T N U O F A R E Z
K J L I N X N H G E W J G V R
```

BANNEKER
CARVER
DREW
ELEVATOR
ELKINS
FOUNTAINPEN
HIRAMREVELS
INVENTIONS
JJLOVE
PENCILSHARPENER
PURVIS
REFRIGERATOR
SCIENCE
STANDARD
THURGOOD

Hint: Words can be horizontal, vertical, backwards or diagonal.

What Am I? The Inventions

SAG KASM

RAIH RAEC

RETRAIGOERRF

NAMACLA

NOENINTIV

RARDIALO

LERAEHGTP

PCNELI HEPRENRAS

NAUFITON PNE

TAOPOT SIPHC

RAESL

CEARAM

DOLBO LMBOEI

OTNUASATR

Unscramble each of the clue words.
Copy the letters in the numbered cells to other cells with the same number.

Word Search #4

What Do You Do?

```
U  O  S  B  F  C  R  A  V  A  C  Y  S  E  B
X  M  K  U  Y  B  B  T  U  S  S  M  P  C  C
J  Q  E  I  P  U  R  D  P  E  N  M  C  T  H
Y  G  U  T  M  R  H  E  N  A  R  A  A  M  I
N  O  B  E  L  P  E  A  C  E  P  R  I  Z  E
A  T  M  D  E  G  T  M  P  N  C  G  R  E  F
I  J  N  U  U  O  T  U  E  O  A  A  A  X  O
C  H  D  E  R  Y  B  A  M  C  W  D  T  Z  F
I  Q  B  L  D  L  D  E  T  S  O  O  X  W  S
S  F  Z  C  I  I  D  O  H  T  O  U  I  H  T
Y  D  A  C  C  V  S  I  I  W  O  U  R  E  A
H  V  A  D  I  N  V  E  N  T  O  R  G  T  F
P  N  R  E  G  N  I  S  R  Y  L  D  N  M  F
N  A  I  C  I  T  I  L  O  P  U  I  Y  E  X
Y  S  V  I  M  W  B  O  K  J  O  V  X  M  Y
```

ATTORNEY – CHIEFOFSTAFF – DANCER - DEMOCRAT - GRAMMY - INVENTOR
JUDGE - NOBELPEACEPRIZE - PHYSICIAN - POLITICIAN - PRESIDENT
REPUBLICAN - SENATOR - SINGER - SUPREMECOURT

Crossword Puzzle: The Inventions

Across	Down
5. Revolutionized by George Washington Carver	1. Take your soiled suits here
8. Used by firefighters to avoid smoke inhalation	2. Used to slow down trains
10. Smile and say "cheese"	3. Used to sign contracts
11. Brilliant mathematician for NASA	4. First African American to receive a patent
12. Revolutionized women's hair care	6. Can't eat just one
13. Go here to give blood	7. Goes up or down
14. Removed to help improve eyesight	9. Keeps food cold
16. Used to make pencils pointy	15. Has three colors

Find the Secret Phrase

Cross out the words below to find a hidden message

```
C  K  S  A  M  S  A  G  S  C  T  B  L  G  A
J  A  C  K  S  O  N  A  A  S  N  C  K  O  I
J  S  R  B  T  I  E  T  M  O  E  A  U  A  T
I  A  F  R  T  N  A  U  I  B  D  C  L  L  Q
R  E  M  T  U  R  E  T  O  P  I  I  C  S  C
O  N  A  E  A  T  A  T  L  N  S  T  N  U  M
T  P  T  C  S  R  H  A  A  A  E  P  I  D  S
N  D  T  A  I  E  T  E  Q  P  R  B  B  O  H
E  S  U  P  L  I  N  S  R  Z  P  C  A  Z  N
V  N  S  K  N  S  O  K  S  S  J  R  R  H  H
N  N  I  U  E  L  E  V  A  T  O  R  A  J  A
I  N  M  H  A  P  R  I  N  C  E  N  C  V  F
S  B  C  N  C  R  U  M  B  V  B  O  K  G  U
X  I  G  T  E  N  A  J  B  Z  G  S  H  T  W
R  E  J  A  M  W  R  E  C  O  R  D  S  Y  T
```

AMBITION	BARACK	CARRUTHERS
CATARACTS	CRUMB	ELEVATOR
ELKINS	GASMASK	GOALS
INSPIRATION	INVENTOR	JACKSON
JAMES	JANET	PATENT
PATTI	PLATINUM	PRESIDENT
PRINCE	RECORDS	RICHES
SOLANGE	SUCCESS	

_ _ _ _ _ _   _ _   _ _ _ _ _ _ _ _ _

Did You Know?

Unscramble the tiles to reveal a message.

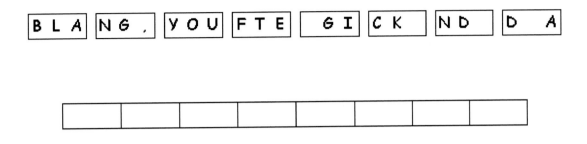

| B L A | N G , | Y O U | F T E | G I | C K | N D | D | A |

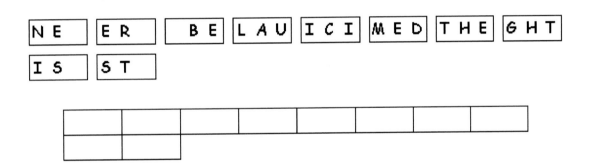

| N E | E R | B E | L A U | I C I | M E D | T H E | G H T |
| I S | S T |

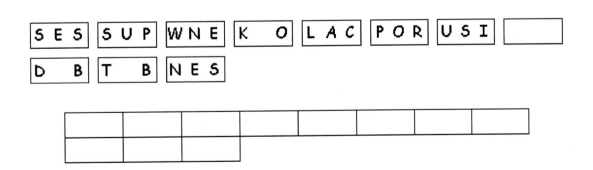

| S E S | S U P | W N E | K | O | L A C | P O R | U S I | |
| D | B | T | B | N E S |

James Brown

Prince

Thomas Elkins

Katherine Johnson

Whitney Houston

Michael Jackson

Taraji P. Henson

Bernie Mac

Thurgood Marshall

Barack Obama

Madame CJ Walker

Oprah Winfrey

Bill Cosby

Denzel Washington

Condoleezza Rice

Word Games (Answers)

Word Search # 1

The Entertainers (Answers)

```
Y  M  C  E  +  +  +  M  +  G  +  +  R  +  Y
H  I  I  +  C  +  +  +  O  +  U  O  +  D  +
P  C  R  S  I  N  G  E  R  O  Y  I  E  +  +
R  H  D  +  +  +  I  +  +  R  N  M  T  +  +
U  A  E  +  +  +  +  R  P  +  O  W  +  A  J
M  E  C  +  +  +  +  D  P  C  +  +  A  A  R
E  L  +  +  B  E  R  N  I  E  M  A  C  L  +
I  +  +  +  +  A  M  +  +  +  +  K  +  +  K
L  +  +  +  H  +  O  +  +  +  S  +  +  +  +
R  +  +  C  +  +  T  +  +  O  +  +  +  +  +
A  +  I  +  +  +  O  +  N  +  +  +  +  +  +
H  R  +  +  +  +  W  +  +  +  +  +  +  +  +
C  +  +  +  +  +  N  +  +  +  +  +  +  +  +
+  +  Y  E  N  T  I  H  W  +  +  +  +  +  +
+  +  +  +  +  +  +  +  +  +  +  +  +  +  +
```

(Over,Down,Direction)
BERNIEMAC (5,7,E)
CEDRIC (3,6,N)
CHARLIEMURPHY (1,13,N)
COMEDY (10,6,NE)
GUITAR (10,1,SE)
JACKSON (15,5,SW)
MICHAEL (2,1,S)
MOONWALK (8,1,SE)
MOTOWN (7,8,S)
PRINCE (9,6,NW)
RICHARDPRYOR (2,12,NE)
SINGER (4,3,E)
WHITNEY (9,14,W)

Who Am I?

Prince	RICNEP	☐☐☐☐☐☐
Guitar	IURATG	☐☐☐☐☐☐
Microphone	HORNIOPEMC	☐☐☐☐☐☐☐☐☐☐ (2)
Musician	SIACUMNI	☐☐☐☐☐☐☐☐ (7)
Television	VOETILISNE	☐☐☐☐☐☐☐☐☐☐ (8)
Grammy	RAGYMM	☐☐☐☐☐☐
Beyoncé	NOBYCEÉ	☐☐☐☐☐☐☐ (9)
Oprah	PORHA	☐☐☐☐☐ (5)
Entertainer	IRNENTEAERT	☐☐☐☐☐☐☐☐☐☐☐
Drummer	RUMMERD	☐☐☐☐☐☐☐
Keyboard	BEAKYROD	☐☐☐☐☐☐☐☐ (3)
Piano	PAINO	☐☐☐☐☐ (1)
Dancing	DIANGNC	☐☐☐☐☐☐☐ (6)
Music	SUIMC	☐☐☐☐☐ (4)
Saxophone	NOXPOHEAS	☐☐☐☐☐☐☐☐☐

J ☐☐☐☐☐☐ F ☐☐☐
  1 2 3 4 5 6   7 8 9

Jackson Five

Crossword Puzzle: The Entertainers (Answers)

Across	Down
2. Most sought after award in the music industry: *GRAMMY*	1. Star of The Color Purple: *WHOOPIGOLDBERG*
8. movie starring Eddie Murphy and Richard Pryor: *HARLEMNIGHTS*	3. Beyoncé's singing group: *DESTINYSCHILD*
10. Popular record label: *MOTOWN*	4. Iconic movie named after a day of the week: *FRIDAY*
11. married Whitney Houston: *BOBBYBROWN*	5. Owner of the 40-40 club: *JAYZ*
12. Has a radio show and several television shows: *STEVEHARVEY*	6. R&B group from Boston: NEW EDITION
14. Prince's favorite color: *PURPLE*	7. Has 88 keys: *PIANO*
	9. Son on the Cosby Show: *THEO*
	10. Michael Jackson's signature move: *MOONWALK*
	13. Popular rapper born in Toronto: *DRAKE*

Who Am I? (Entertainment)

Unscramble the tiles to reveal a famous group

S	A	D I A	S U	R O S	N A	T H E	N D	M E S

P R E

Diana Ross and the Supremes

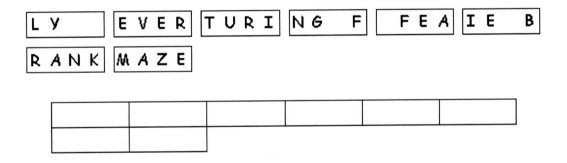

L Y		E V E R	T U R I	N G F	F E A	I E	B

R A N K	M A Z E

Maze Featuring Frankie Beverly

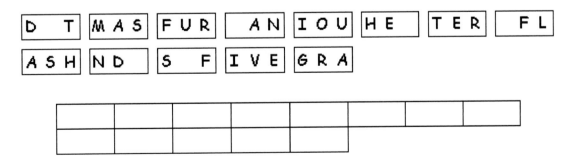

D	T	M A S	F U R		A N	I O U	H E		T E R		F L

A S H	N D	S F	I V E	G R A

Grandmaster Flash and the Furious Five

Word Search # 2 (Answers)
Actors and Muscians

```
T A R A J I P H E N S O N A A
R O Y R P D R A H C I R + C +
K J + Y + + + S O + + T A Y
C A H + A + + + E O + O + D D
A M + A + D + + R K R + E E O
B E + + R + G + U I + M + M O
Y S + + + L + N G E O + + Y W
A B D + + + E Y I C + + + A Y
P R + E + + O M F N + + + W L
G O + + N B + O N + I + + A L
I W + + Y Z S + E I + A + R O
B N + B + G E + D + G + R D H
+ + A + N + + L D + + H + T +
+ B + I + E M P I R E + T + +
+ + K Y M M E + H + + + + S +
```

(Over, Down, Direction)

ACADEMYAWARD (14,1,S)   ACTOR (15,1,SW)
BABYBOY (2,14,NE)   BIGPAYBACK (1,12,N)
COOKIE (10,2,S)   DENZEL (3,8,SE)
EMMY (7,15,W)   **EMPIRE (6,14,E)**
HARLEMNIGHTS (3,4,SE)   HIDDENFIGURES (9,15,N)
HOLLYWOOD (15,12,N)   JAMESBROWN (2,3,S)
KINGSOFCOMEDY (3,15,NE)   RICHARDPRYOR (12,2,W)
TARAJIPHENSON (1,1,E)   TRAININGDAY (14,13,NW)

Discover the Phrase (answers)

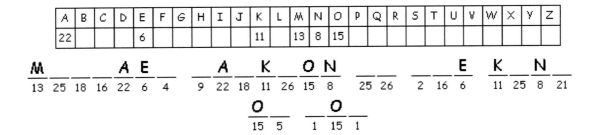

A	B	C	D	E	F	G	H	I	J	K	L	M	N	O	P	Q	R	S	T	U	V	W	X	Y	Z
22				6						11		13	8	15											

Michael Jackson is the King of Pop

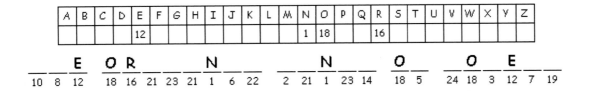

A	B	C	D	E	F	G	H	I	J	K	L	M	N	O	P	Q	R	S	T	U	V	W	X	Y	Z
				12									1	18		16									

The Original Kings of Comedy

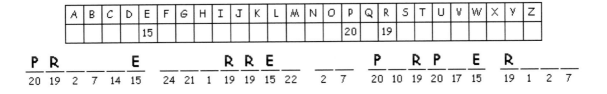

A	B	C	D	E	F	G	H	I	J	K	L	M	N	O	P	Q	R	S	T	U	V	W	X	Y	Z
				15											20		19								

Prince Starred in Purple Rain

Word Search #3

The History-Makers (Answers)

```
P  +  S  +  +  P  +  D  R  +  +  +  +  +  R
+  E  +  N  U  +  O  +  E  +  +  +  S  +  E
S  +  N  R  O  O  S  +  F  +  +  +  C  H  K
+  T  V  C  G  I  +  N  R  +  +  +  I  E  E
+  I  A  R  I  +  T  +  I  +  +  R  E  V  N
S  +  U  N  +  L  +  N  G  K  A  +  N  O  N
+  H  +  W  D  +  S  +  E  M  L  +  C  L  A
T  R  E  V  R  A  C  H  R  V  +  E  E  J  B
+  R  +  +  +  +  R  E  A  +  N  +  +  J  +
D  +  +  +  +  +  V  D  T  R  +  I  +  +  +
+  +  +  +  +  E  +  +  O  +  P  +  +  +  +
+  +  +  +  L  +  +  +  R  +  +  E  +  +  +
+  +  +  S  E  L  E  V  A  T  O  R  N  +  +
N  E  P  N  I  A  T  N  U  O  F  +  +  E  +
+  +  +  +  +  +  +  +  +  +  +  +  +  +  R
```

(Over,Down,Direction)
BANNEKER(15,8,N)
CARVER(7,8,W)
DREW(1,10,NE)
ELEVATOR(5,13,E)
ELKINS(12,8,NW)
FOUNTAINPEN(11,14,W)
HIRAMREVELS(14,3,SW)
INVENTIONS(12,10,NW)
JJLOVE(14,9,N)
PENCILSHARPENER(1,1,SE)
PURVIS(6,1,SW)
REFRIGERATOR(9,1,S)
SCIENCE(13,2,S)
STANDARD(1,3,SE)
THURGOOD (1,8,NE)

What Am I? The Inventions

Gas mask — SAG KASM

Hair care — RAIH RAEC

Refrigerator — RETRAIGOERRF

Almanac — NAMACLA

Invention — NOENINTIV

Railroad — RARDIALO

Telegraph — LERAEHGTP

Pencil sharpener — PCNELI HEPRENRAS

Fountain pen — NAUFITON PNE

Potato chips — TAOPOT SIPHC

Laser — RAESL

Camera — CEARAM

Blood mobile — DOLBO LMBOEI

Astronaut — OTNUASATR

Bonus Word:

Traffic signal

Word Search #4

What Do You Do?

```
+  +  S  +  +  +  +  +  +  +  +  Y  +  +  +
+  +  +  U  +  +  +  +  +  +  S  M  +  +  C
+  +  +  +  P  +  R  +  +  E  +  M  +  T  H
+  +  +  +  R  +  E  N  +  R  A  A  +  I
N  O  B  E  L  P  E  A  C  E  P  R  I  Z  E
A  T  +  +  +  +  T  M  P  N  C  G  +  +  F
I  +  N  +  +  O  +  U  E  O  A  +  +  +  O
C  +  +  E  R  +  B  A  M  C  +  D  +  +  F
I  +  +  +  D  L  +  E  T  +  O  +  +  +  S
S  +  +  +  I  I  D  +  +  T  +  U  +  +  T
Y  +  +  C  +  +  S  +  +  +  O  +  R  E  A
H  +  A  +  I  N  V  E  N  T  O  R  G  T  F
P  N  R  E  G  N  I  S  R  +  +  D  N  +  F
N  A  I  C  I  T  I  L  O  P  U  +  +  E  +
+  +  +  +  +  +  +  +  +  J  +  +  +  +  Y
```

(Over, Down, Direction)
ATTORNEY (8,8,SE)
CHIEFOFSTAFF (15,2,S)
DANCER 12,8,NW)
DEMOCRAT (7,10,NE)
GRAMMY(12,6,N)
INVENTOR (5,12,E)
JUDGE (10,15,NE)
NOBELPEACEPRIZE (1,5,E)
PHYSICIAN (1,13,N)
POLITICIAN (10,14,W)
PRESIDENT (10,14,NW)
REPUBLICAN (11,4,SW)
SENATOR (11,2,SW)
SINGER (8,13,W)
SUPREMECOURT (3,1,SE)

Crossword Puzzle: The Inventions (Solutions)

Across	Down
5. Revolutionized by George Washington Carver: *PEANUT*	**1. Take your soiled suits here** *DRYCLEANERS*
8. Used by firefighters to avoid smoke inhalation *GASMASK*	**2. Used to slow down trains** *AIRBRAKE*
10. Smile and say "cheese" *CAMERA*	**3. Used to sign contracts** *FOUNTAINPEN*
11. Brilliant mathematician for NASA *KATHERINEJOHNSON*	**4. First African American to receive a patent** *THOMASJENNINGS*
12. Revolutionized women's hair care *CJWALKER*	**6. Can't eat just one** *POTATOCHIPS*
13. Go here to give blood *BLOODMOBILE*	**7. Goes up or down** *ELAVATOR*
14. Removed to help improve eyesight *CATARACTS*	**9. Keeps food cold** *REFRIGERATOR*
16. Used to make pencils pointy *PENCILSHARPENER*	**15. Has three colors** *TRAFFICLIGHT*

Find the Secret Phrase

Cross out the words below to find a hidden message (answers)

```
C  K  S  A  M  S  A  G  S  C  T  B  L  G  A
J  A  C  K  S  O  N  A  A  S  N  C  K  O  I
J  S  R  B  T  I  E  T  M  O  E  A  U  A  T
I  A  F  R  T  N  A  U  I  B  D  C  L  L  +
R  +  M  T  U  R  E  T  +  P  I  +  C  S  +
O  +  A  E  A  T  A  T  L  +  S  T  +  U  +
T  P  +  C  S  R  H  A  A  +  E  +  I  +  S
N  +  T  +  I  E  T  E  +  P  R  +  B  O  +
E  S  +  P  L  I  +  S  R  +  P  +  A  +  N
V  +  S  K  N  S  O  +  +  S  +  +  R  +  +
N  I  U  E  L  E  V  A  T  O  R  A  +  +
I  N  M  H  A  P  R  I  N  C  E  +  C  +  +
S  +  C  N  C  R  U  M  B  +  +  +  K  +  +
+  I  G  T  E  N  A  J  +  +  +  +  +  +  +
R  E  +  +  +  +  R  E  C  O  R  D  S  +  +
```

(Over, Down, Direction)

AMBITION (8,2,SE)   BARACK (13,8,S)   CARRUTHERS (1,1,SE)
CATARACTS (10,1,SW)   CRUMB (5,13,E)   ELEVATOR (5,11,E)
ELKINS (6,8,SW)   GASMASK (8,1,W)   GOALS (14,1,S)
INSPIRATION (1,12,NE)   INVENTOR (1,12,N)   JACKSON(1,2,E)
JAMES (1,3,SE)   JANET(8,14,W)   PATENT (10,8,NW)
PATTI (2,7,NE)   PLATINUM (10,5,SW)   PRESIDENT(11,9,N)
PRINCE (6,12,E)   RECORDS (7,15,E)   RICHES (1,15,NE)
SOLANGE (8,9,SW)   SUCCESS (15,7,NW)

Answer:

Black is Beautiful

Did You Know? (Answers)

B L A	N G ,	Y O U	F T E	G I	C K	N D	D A

"Young, gifted and black."

N E	E R	B E	L A U	I C I	M E D	T H E	G H T
I S	S T

"Laughter is the best medicine."

S E S	S U P	W N E	K O	L A C	P O R	U S I	
D B	T B	N E S

"Support black owned businesses."

About the Artist

David Sanders is owner of Cross2infinity art studios. He was born in 1970 in Winona, Mississippi. His family moved to Chicago while he was still an infant. He developed a love for art and comics at the age of seven and has pursued it ever since. Honing his craft under the tutelage of Mr. Sherman Beck at Dunbar high school, David won awards for logo design and is still creating great art and comics today. His specialty is portraits, graphic design, and digital and wet mediums.

About the Author

Jeffrey White is a former financial advisor turned best-selling author, motivational speaker, freelance writer, wellness coach, triathlete and personal trainer. He lives in Florida with his wife Monica and son Little Jeffrey. He is from Chicago, Illinois and graduated from Illinois State University with a degree in Business Administration. www.JeffWhiteFitnessSolutions.com

JEFF WHITE FITNESS SOLUTIONS LLC.

HAVE A FITNESS PROBLEM? LET'S FIND A FITNESS SOLUTION!

https://www.youtube.com/user/JWFitness1

Jeffrey has written several self-help and inspirational books, designed to help a person become the best they can be in several key aspects of their lives:

<u>Readi - Set Go! A Simple Guide to Establishing a Successful Small Business.</u>

Co-written with Stephanie A. Wynn

Do you dream of owning your own business but don't know where to begin? Does the thought of being self-employed excite you, but scare you at the same time? Do you have an intense desire to run your own successful business? Are you tired of waiting on someone to give you a job and want to create one instead?

Starting a business is difficult, but it's not impossible. Gain valuable insight on the start-up process and running a successful business with this step by step guide. Learn about the critical first steps that many overlook when starting a business.

Are you READI to create a solid, reputable company that no one can take from you?

<u>Success Principles 101: A Step By Step Guide on Setting and Achieving Goals.</u>

The first book in the "Success" series: Are you ready for success? Setting goals is simple, accomplishing them is not. In this easy to read guide, we identify the pitfalls that many encounter while attempting to achieve their goals and how to overcome them.

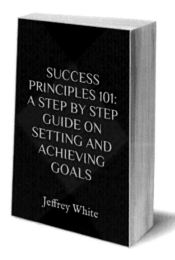

The Diet of Success: Healthy Eating Tips for Hard Working Professionals.

While many people think money is the key to happiness and prosperity, it's all irrelevant without good health. When it comes to success, many of us are willing to do anything to get it. Unfortunately, that often includes sacrificing our health and overall well-being.

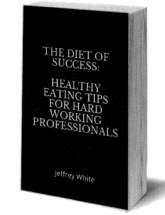

The first line of defense against illness is not medicine from the doctor but the foods we eat. The effort it takes to be successful can take a tremendous toll on the body. By knowing which foods to eat (and avoid), a person can focus all their energies on setting and achieving goals instead of which medicines they need to take to make it through the day.

Cancer, diabetes, obesity, high blood pressure, and other ailments are near epidemic levels in today's society. Are pesticides, GMO's, artificial food colorings and other things added to our foods the culprit? Discover how many of the foods we eat today may be the reason behind so many of our health issues. Understand how a slight change in diet can not only keep us healthy, but provide the energy we need to achieve all our goals.

The foods we eat can either help us or hurt us. If you're working long hours and trying to make a better life for yourself, eating the proper foods can give you the energy not to make your dreams come true, but to let you enjoy the fruits of your labor for years to come.

The 3 Pillars of Strength: Increasing Your Physical, Mental and Spiritual Fitness.

In order to become the best you can be, it's important to work on all aspects of your life, together. It's time for YOU to reach your FULL potential.

It's time to tap into ALL your unique traits and talents that can propel you to greatness.

It's time to face all the challenges and obstacles this world will throw at you with the quiet confidence that you CAN and WILL overcome.

It's time to understand that, at your disposal, you have the tools needed to succeed! Available in paperback, Audible and Kindle formats on Amazon.

Don't Miss Any Of The Books In The Yes We Did! Series:

Yes We Did! Amazing Accomplishments In African American History
Volume I

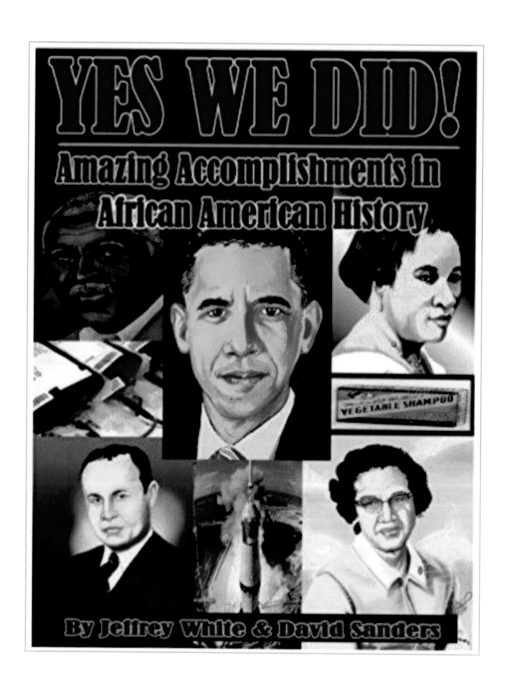

Coming Soon:

Yes We Did! The Revolutionaries

Angela Davis

Made in the USA
Middletown, DE
04 March 2018